LAUREL-LEAF
BOOKS

An unsolved case is the most intriguing kind of mystery. The clues are there, but the solution remains hidden. The reader becomes the detective, sifting through the facts just as the police do in trying to solve the case. And perhaps some sharp-eyed reader will find a clue that holds the answer to one of these three unsolved crimes.

ARNOLD MADISON is a successful author of children's books. He is a free-lance writer and teacher of creative writing.

THE LAUREL-LEAF LIBRARY brings together under a single imprint outstanding works of fiction and nonfiction particularly suitable for young adult readers, both in and out of the classroom. This series is under the editorship of Charles F. Reasoner, Professor of Elementary Education, New York University.

# GREAT
# UNSOLVED
# CASES

## BY
## ARNOLD MADISON

## ILLUSTRATED BY
## MICHAEL DEAS

LAUREL-LEAF
BOOKS

Published by
Dell Publishing Co., Inc.
1 Dag Hammarskjold Plaza
New York, New York 10017

Photographs courtesy of:

Bettmann Archive, p. 48;
Radio Times Hulton Picture Library, pp. 8, 12, 24;
United Press International, p. 34;
Wide World Photos, pp. 38, 50.

Laurel-Leaf Library ® TM 766734, Dell Publishing Co., Inc.

ISBN: 0-440-93099-5

Reprinted by arrangement with Franklin Watts, Inc.

Printed in the United States of America
First Laurel-Leaf printing — April 1980

# CONTENTS

# CHAPTER 1

# THE
# LURE OF
# UNSOLVED
# CASES

Both young and old readers enjoy reading about unsolved cases. There are several reasons. First, we all like to be detectives. We read these cases and try to solve them.

There is another reason we like true crime stories. Mystery stories and books are very popular. An unsolved case is like a mystery story. But the author cannot tell who did it. No one can do that. So we hunt for clues as we read. Sometimes we think we know the answer.

True unsolved crimes also show that police work is hard. The police can do wonders at times. They find criminals from only a few clues. Sometimes they do not catch the person. That means there were not enough clues. Or the clues were confusing. That does not mean the criminals were smart. Our courts want to protect everyone. They will not find someone guilty unless there is much evidence. Nobody wants innocent people put into prison.

There are three unsolved cases in this book. See if you can pick out the guilty person. You may discover something nobody else has found.

# CHAPTER 2

# JACK
# THE
# RIPPER

The facts are simple. Between August 31 and November 9, 1888, five women were murdered in London. There were other killings at that time, also. But these five persons were all murdered by the same killer. After the fifth murder, there were no more killings by this person.

No one knows who did the murders. Or why the women were killed. Or even why the murderer stopped. Almost a hundred years have gone by since the crimes. The answers are still unknown.

The case was shocking. A whole country talked about the murders. Now the world knows about Jack the Ripper. He was called this because the victims were badly cut with a knife. Plays and books have been written about Jack. There are even "Ripper" clubs. The members meet and talk about the case. Each person has his or her own explanation. Yet—no one knows for certain who committed those murders in London's East End.

The East End of London was the poor part of the city. In 1888, 900,000 people lived there. Most had no jobs. People died from the cold and a lack

*Women living in the East End
looked with fear at any stranger.*

of food. Families were crowded into tiny rooms. For example, a five-member family lived in one musty cellar room. Four pigs shared the room with them.

The buildings were old and many had broken windows. Filth and blood from slaughterhouses filled the streets. Coal smoke from chimneys mixed with the fog. At times, the smog was so thick that a person could see only a few feet ahead.

Other Britons paid no attention to the East End. It was as if they wanted to forget those poor people. Jack the Ripper changed that.

Early on Friday morning, August 31, 1888, George Cross was on his way to work. The sun was not up yet. The streets were dark and damp. The only light was a gas lamp at the far end of the street. He spotted a bundle of rags in an alley. When he looked at them, he saw they were the body of a woman. She had been stabbed to death.

Cross looked around. The streets were quiet at this early hour. The murderer must be gone. Cross didn't hear footsteps or a horse-drawn cab.

*Was this woman to be
Jack the Ripper's next victim?*

The police learned the victim's name was Polly Nichols. She had been murdered on the spot. But why hadn't she screamed? How had the murderer escaped so easily? One reason was that people would not notice a man who had blood on his clothes. Many such people could be seen in the East End. They worked for the many slaughterhouses.

A week later the second body was found. Annie Chapman was killed in the same way as Polly Nichols. Her body was found in the back hallway of a boarding house. Seventeen people slept in that house. But none had heard anything. A woman had seen Annie earlier that night. Annie was standing outside the house. She was talking to a man about forty years old who wore a hunting hat.

Annie and Polly were alike in some ways. They walked the streets at night, looking for men to buy them drinks. They often stayed in bars until very late. Walking home along the dark, empty streets, they had met Jack the Ripper.

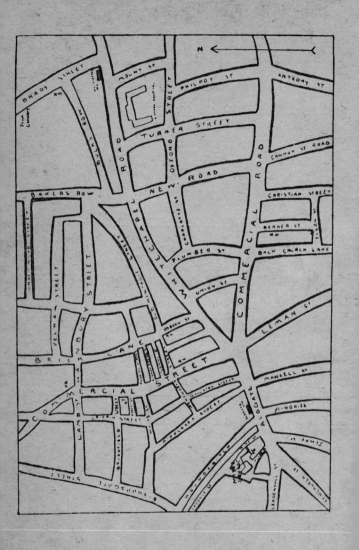

*A map of London's East End*

The police knew the murder weapon was a long knife. The blade was thin and narrow. It was at least 6 to 8 inches (15.2 to 20.3 cm) long. A knife like this might be used by a cork-cutter or shoemaker. The weapon had not been found at either murder. But there was one clue. The police thought Jack the Ripper might be a doctor. The bodies were badly slashed. But the cuts had been done by someone who knew the human body. The murderer knew just where to find the veins and arteries.

Newspapers printed many stories about the murders. People all over England began talking and thinking about the East End. This was one good thing caused by the murders. A nation was shocked. And many people wanted to improve the East End. They said it was not right for poor people to live that way. Groups began trying to make the East End a better place. More police now walked the streets. But Jack the Ripper was not yet finished. His next attack was to be even more horrible.

*Jack the Ripper had struck again.*

Two weeks went by. Everyone waited to see if Jack would strike again. Suspects were questioned and then released. Everyone had an alibi. A city and nation held its breath, afraid another murder would happen.

In the early hours of September 30, a man was going to a club. He turned his pony cart into a courtyard. Suddenly the pony stopped. The man looked down. He could not see what made the pony stop. Checking more closely, he saw a woman's body. She was either dead or drunk.

The man called people from the club. They turned the woman over. Her clothes were wet. But her body was still warm. Some red and white flowers were pinned to her black jacket.

The police began a search. They talked to everyone at the club. But suddenly they had to stop their investigation. Another body had been found.

Jack the Ripper seemed to think no one could catch him. This fourth murder was done in a public square. Three streets ran into that square. He

*Jack the Ripper's second victim had been seen
with a man shortly before her death.*

might easily have been seen. This square was checked every fifteen minutes at night. A policeman had walked through there at 1:30 A.M. The square was empty. At 1:45 A.M. he found the woman's body.

Some people had seen the woman earlier. Two of them said she was with a man. They said the man was middle-aged and was wearing a hunting cap. The man seen with the second victim had looked much the same.

The double killing in one night caused a panic. People all over London became frightened. What if Jack the Ripper came to their part of the city? Many people thought the police were not doing a good job. They wanted the chief of police to give up his post.

Newspapers called the police stupid. Why didn't they catch this terrible murderer?

The London police did not have the tools that police use today. They could not take fingerprints. They did not know how to perform blood tests. There were only two ways to capture a criminal. They had to catch him or her doing the crime. Or

*Elizabeth Prater thought she
heard a cry in the night.*

an informer had to tell who and where the criminal was. No one saw Jack the Ripper or knew anything about him.

Many people thought they knew. A thousand letters a day arrived at police headquarters. Some persons claimed to have seen Jack the Ripper. Others said they were Jack. These letters did not help the police in their search for Jack.

On November 9, 1888, Jack the Ripper killed his last victim. This crime was different from the others.

Mary Jane Kelly lived in a boarding house on Dorset Street. Elizabeth Prater rented the room directly above Mary Jane Kelly's. Elizabeth Prater went to bed at about 1:30 A.M. Between three and four o'clock, she was awakened by her cat. At the same time she heard a low cry somewhere in the house.

"Oh, murder!" someone cried.

She waited but heard nothing more. Elizabeth Prater went back to sleep. Nighttime sounds were common in the house.

About 10:45 A.M., there was a knock on

*The police looked for clues that would tell them who murdered Mary Jane Kelly.*

Mary Jane's door. The landlord had sent someone to get the rent money. When Mary Jane did not open the door, the man went to a window and looked in. He found Jack the Ripper's fifth victim.

Mary Jane Kelly was not killed on the street. She was murdered in her room. The killing was like the other crimes. The same type weapon had been used. Mary Jane Kelly was a streetwalker. Her body had been badly slashed.

When the police arrived, they found ashes in the fireplace. The coals were still warm. The fire had been very hot. The flames had burned the handle off a tea kettle. But why had Jack the Ripper set a fire?

Sifting the ashes, the police found a few pieces of cloth. A friend had given Mary Jane Kelly some old clothing. Jack the Ripper might have burned them. But why? Also, cloth does not burn easily. Something would have to be added to the fire to make the flames so hot. Some say Jack the Ripper lit the fire for light. He would need to see the body he was slashing. But he could have used candles that were in the room. Perhaps police

*Few people dared to walk the dark streets of London because of Jack the Ripper.*

science today might have found other clues in those ashes.

Why did Jack the Ripper change his pattern? Why did this crime happen inside a building? Why did he set a strange fire?

During the next few months, murders were committed in the East End. At first the police thought Jack the Ripper did some of them. But soon they knew the murders were not the same as the five other killings. Months and then a year went by. Jack never struck again. Nor did the police ever find the person behind the crimes. The police commissioner resigned.

Lots of people like to study famous crimes. They have their own ideas about Jack the Ripper. Some of them have made lists of possible suspects. These are people that the police did not suspect at the time of the murders.

For example, some people say that Thomas Neill Cream was Jack the Ripper. Cream was a man who poisoned streetwalkers. He was later hanged. As the rope was placed around his neck, he started to speak.

*Some people thought Albert Victor,*
*Duke of Clarence, was Jack the Ripper.*

"I'm Jack the—"

The trapdoor opened, and Cream was dead. Some people believe he was going to confess to the five murders. But Cream was in prison when the murders happened. Also, murderers usually use the same methods. It would be odd for someone who used poison to switch to stabbing.

One person wrote a book about Jack the Ripper. He said Jack was the eldest son of the future King Edward VII. The son's name was Albert Victor. His title was Duke of Clarence. The author said the royal family knew that Albert was insane. He thought that the royal family stopped the police from arresting Albert.

Albert is said to have died in the flu epidemic of 1892. The author thinks the royal family made up this story. Albert may have been placed in a mental hospital. But Albert is a poor choice as Jack the Ripper. He is known to have been in Scotland when the first murders happened.

Another suspect was Frank Miles. He was a well-known painter in London. He would use streetwalkers as models for his paintings. And he and Albert knew each other. He supposedly died in 1887. This was a year before the murders. But new evidence showed he died in 1891.

Another possible Jack the Ripper died one month after the last murder. The suspect, Montague John Druitt, was a failure. He was a poor law student and teacher. In December, 1888, he jumped into the River Thames and drowned. Did he kill himself because he murdered five women? Most people think he killed himself because he knew he was going insane.

There is still one more possibility about the real Jack the Ripper. Was Jack the Ripper actually Jill the Ripper? Could some woman have hated other women so much that she killed them? Possibly Jill the Ripper was a nurse who knew about the human body.

Many questions are left unanswered. Why did the murders stop so suddenly? Was Jack arrested for another crime and put in prison? Was Jack himself killed by someone? Or did he kill himself?

It will not be too long before the London police close the case of Jack the Ripper. Unsolved cases are left open for one hundred years in England. Even when the case is closed, that will not be the end. People will continue talking and wondering about Jack the Ripper.

# CHAPTER 3

# THE

# LINDBERGH

# KIDNAPPING

The news swept around the world like a tidal wave. The Lindbergh baby had been kidnapped!

In March, 1932, Charles A. Lindbergh was one of the most famous men anywhere. Five years before, he had flown across the Atlantic Ocean. He had been the first to do it nonstop and alone. He was a hero. Almost every country named something after him. Later he married Anne Morrow. Their first son was born in 1930 and was named Charles, Jr.

The Lindberghs lived on an estate in New Jersey. On March 1, 1932, Charles came home from work as usual. Anne did not feel well. Charles, Jr. was asleep in his upstairs bedroom. He had a cold. A few minutes after nine, Charles and Anne were in the living room.

Suddenly Charles looked around. "What was that?"

Charles had heard a sound like wood breaking. He and Anne listened for a few moments. But there were no more sounds. A little later Anne went to her room. Charles worked in the library.

At ten o'clock, the baby's nurse, Betty Gow,

*Charles A. Lindbergh as he looked in 1932.*

went to see if Charles, Jr. was all right. She did not turn on a light. She did not want to wake the baby. She let her eyes get used to the dark. She felt carefully around the crib. The child was gone.

Betty went to Anne's room. "Mrs. Lindbergh, do you have the baby?"

"Why, no, I don't have the baby."

Charles raced upstairs. He checked the crib. Two large pins were still in the blankets. The baby's nurse had pinned the blankets to the mattress. The pins would have stopped Charles, Jr. from climbing out of the crib. Someone had taken the baby from the crib.

"Anne," Charles said, "they have stolen our baby."

An envelope lay on a radiator by the window. Lindbergh did not touch it. There might be fingerprints.

The police were called. While they waited, Anne and the nurse searched the house. They looked in every room. The baby was not in the house. Lindbergh got his rifle. He and the butler drove around the estate. They found nothing.

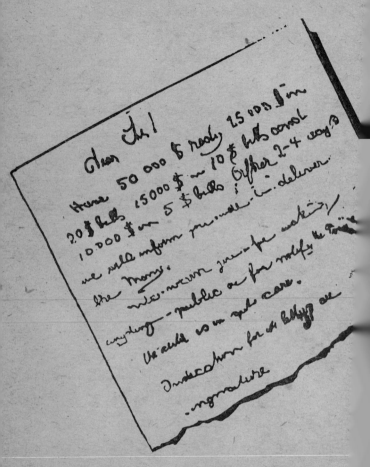

*A ransom note was one of the clues.*

When the police came, they started their own search. Clues were found under the nursery window. There was a smudged footprint and two holes in the ground. The police found other clues. A ladder lay nearby in the grass. The ladder had been built by hand. One rung was broken.

Charles remembered the sound he had heard earlier. The kidnapper must have stepped on that rung while holding the baby. The weight was too much. The rung had snapped.

The envelope was checked for fingerprints. There were none on it or on the note inside. The ransom letter demanded $50,000. The kidnapper would phone in two to four days. The note said Charles must not call the police. It also said that Charles should not tell the newspapers. It was too late to stop that. The news was out.

There was something odd about the writing in the note. Words were misspelled. *Gut* was written for good, and *anyding* for anything. The police wondered if a foreigner had written the note. There was a sign drawn at the bottom. Two circles overlapped. Where they met, there was an oval.

Three holes in a straight line were punched through each part.

By the next morning, newspapers across the world carried the news. The police set up headquarters in the estate garage. Hundreds of reporters and onlookers stayed outside the gates. Thousands of phone calls came in on the twenty telephones in the garage.

There were offers of help. One was from the famous gangster Al Capone, who was in prison. He offered $10,000 as a reward. The money would go to anyone who found the baby. Capone secretly tried to make a deal with a New York City newspaper. If the paper could get him free, Capone would help search for the baby. The offer was turned down.

The police began their search. But they did not want to scare the kidnapper. Once the baby was safe, they would work harder. The police did wonder if the kidnapping was an inside job. One clue seemed to show that.

The Lindberghs spent weekends at their estate. But they would stay with Anne's mother during the week. This weekend the baby had caught a cold. So the Lindberghs stayed at their own home all week. How did the kidnapper know they would be there on Tuesday night? How did the kidnapper know how to find the baby's room?

The police questioned the nurse. They also questioned the cook and butler. Charles said these people were innocent. He thought an underworld gang had carried out the kidnapping.

Charles, Jr. was sick and needed special medicine. Charles and Anne were worried about the baby's health. To help them, newspapers across the country printed the diet and the special medicine the baby would need.

A letter arrived on March 4. The envelope had been mailed in Brooklyn, New York. At the bottom of the letter was the strange design. The same one had been on the first ransom note. The kidnapper now wanted $70,000. Again words were misspelled. *Gut* for good. And the word *aus* appeared. Both were German words. Was the kidnapper a German-born person? The note kept saying "we." Was there a gang, as Lindbergh thought?

# WANTED

## INFORMATION AS TO THE WHEREABOUTS OF

## CHAS. A. LINDBERGH, Jr.

### OF HOPEWELL, N. J.

## SON OF COL. CHAS. A. LINDBERGH

**World-Famous Aviator**

**This child was kidnaped from his home in Hopewell, N. J., between 8 and 10 p. m. on Tuesday, March 1, 1932.**

### DESCRIPTION:

| | |
|---|---|
| Age, 20 months | Hair, blond, curly |
| Weight, 27 to 30 lbs. | Eyes, dark blue |
| Height, 29 inches | Complexion, light |

**Deep dimple in center of chin**
**Dressed in one-piece coverall night suit**

ADDRESS ALL COMMUNICATIONS TO
COL. H. N. SCHWARZKOPF, TRENTON, N. J., or
COL. CHAS. A. LINDBERGH, HOPEWELL, N. J.

ALL COMMUNICATIONS WILL BE TREATED IN CONFIDENCE

March 11, 1932

COL. H. NORMAN SCHWARZKOPF
Supt. New Jersey State Police, Trenton, N. J.

*A police poster asked for news about the Lindbergh baby.*

The letter also said the baby was well. But the kidnapper wanted the police to stop their search. Nothing would be done until the news stopped appearing in the newspapers.

Another letter arrived a few days later. At the bottom of the page was the same design. Only the police, the Lindberghs, and the kidnapper knew about that. The letter repeated the demand for $70,000.

A man unknown to the police and the Lindberghs wanted to help them. His name was Dr. John Condon. He was seventy-four years old and lived in the Bronx, New York. Charles Lindbergh was a hero to him.

Condon read a newspaper called the Bronx *Home News*. He was a friend of the paper's owner. So Condon put a small ad in the Bronx *Home News*. He offered to pay $1,000 of his own money to the kidnappers. He also offered to act as a go-between.

The next night John Condon received a letter. The note told him what to do when Lindbergh had the money. There was another envelope for

Charles Lindbergh. Condon called him. Lindbergh asked the man to come to see him.

The second letter said the baby was 150 miles (241 km) away. When Lindbergh handed over the money, they would give him the address. First, they wanted the money. Eight hours later Lindbergh would get the address. The secret symbol was at the bottom of the letter.

Lindbergh got the money. An ad was put in the New York *American*—MONEY IS READY. On the night of March 11, Condon received a phone call. The deep voice had a strong accent. Condon thought the man was German. The caller spoke with another person in the background. This person answered in Italian. The first man said Dr. Condon would hear from the gang again.

Eight-thirty the next night, Condon's doorbell rang. A taxi driver gave him a letter. Condon was to go to a food market in the Bronx. He was to bring the money with him. There would be another note for him at the market. Condon did not have the money yet. But he wanted to meet the kidnapper.

The directions brought him to Woodlawn Cemetery in the Bronx. The place was cold and dark. Someone waved a white handkerchief through the bars of the fence. Condon saw a dim figure. A cloth hid most of the man's face.

"Did you get the money?" the man asked.

Condon knew the voice. That was the German-sounding man he had talked to earlier.

"No. I couldn't bring the money until I saw the package." *Package* meant the kidnapped baby.

They both heard footsteps. The man leaped over the high fence. He thought Condon had brought the police. He raced along the street and into a park. Condon ran after him, catching up to the man.

The stranger was scared. "Would I burn if the baby is dead?"

Dead? thought Condon. What did the kidnapper mean? The masked stranger told him the baby was fine. No one should worry.

"You know my name," Condon said. "What is yours?"

"John."

*Condon ran into the park after John.*

"Are you a German?"

"No, Scandinavian."

Condon again said he would give the man $1,000 of his own money. But the man said, "We don't want your money." Condon wondered how many others were part of the plot.

John said there were six people. He was afraid of them. They would get him if he left. The kidnapping had been planned for a year.

Condon told him a newspaper notice would be printed when the money was ready. John said he would send the baby's sleeping suit to Condon. That would prove that Condon was dealing with the right person.

Four days passed before the sleeping suit arrived. Lindbergh checked it carefully. He was sure it was the suit his son had been wearing. At least they now knew they were in touch with the true kidnapper.

A week went by. More letters came from the kidnapper. But no firm deal was set. The money was ready. Each serial number had been noted. By doing this, the police could learn where the money was spent.

*The kidnapper waited for Condon and Lindbergh at Saint Raymond's Cemetery.*

Finally, April 2 was agreed on as the date to hand over the money. Lindbergh went to Condon's house. The hours passed slowly. At eight o'clock, a cab driver brought a letter. The kidnapper said everything was ready. St. Raymond's Cemetery in the Bronx was to be the meeting place.

Condon and Lindbergh drove there. Charles remained in the car. Condon walked along the street.

A voice called from the dark cemetery. "Here, Doctor."

It was John, who demanded the money. Condon told him that Lindbergh could get only $50,000 and not $70,000.

John thought about this. Then he said, "Well, all right. I suppose if we can't get seventy, we get fifty."

But Condon wanted a note telling how to find the baby. Finally, John said he would go to get the note. Condon would return to the car and get the money.

Condon told Lindbergh what had happened. They removed $20,000 from the box of money, leaving only $50,000. Taking the money, Condon went to the cemetery. The kidnapper returned in thirteen minutes. This might mean that his home was nearby. John gave Condon a note. Then Condon handed over the ransom money.

The note said the baby was on a 28-foot (8.5 m) boat named *Nelly*. The boat was near Gay Head, Massachusetts. Lindbergh flew to Massachusetts.

For a day and a half, he searched for the boat. No boat named *Nelly* could be found. Condon put ads in the newspaper, asking better directions. Nine more days passed. There was no further word from the kidnapper.

Lindbergh asked the federal government for help. The Treasury Department had a list of the ransom bills' serial numbers. The list was sent to stores and banks.

In Newark, New Jersey, a bank teller saw the list. The money added up to $50,000. He knew the Lindbergh kidnapper had demanded that much money. He told a friend who was a reporter for the Newark *News*. The reporter decided Lindbergh must have paid the money. But the baby was still missing. A story appeared in the *News*. Other newspapers printed the story. Lindbergh was angry. He was afraid the kidnappers might harm the baby.

Everything changed on May 12. A man walking in the woods near the Lindbergh home found a baby's body. The baby's clothing matched Charles, Jr.'s clothes. The baby had been dead for more than two months. He might even have died the night of the kidnapping. Death was caused by a fractured skull.

Now nothing stopped the police in their search. Only three clues would help them: the ransom notes, the ladder, and the numbers on the ransom money.

The handwriting on the notes was probably disguised. But the spelling was by a foreign-born person. Condon had thought John was German. A large population of German people lived in the Bronx. John read the Bronx *Home News*. This paper was sold mainly in the Bronx.

The ladder was sent to a wood expert. The

# New York Times.

Copyright, 1932, by The New York Times Company.

NEW YORK, FRIDAY, MAY 13, 1932.

TWO CENTS In New York | THREE CENTS | FOUR CENTS Elsewhere

## 3-Point Relief Plan 0,000 to Use as Loans

to Put the Proposal Before Colleagues—
Would Help States Handle Jobless
Money for Spurring Business.

**ARTHUR KROCK**

*Special to The New York Times.*

—President
nominates Watson
in lead-
their
ral re-
private
prises
iotating
nalities,
lieves
of mor-
ief of

port agricultural aid, and the re-
maining $1,180,000,000 issued to
private business for reproductive
enterprises, assured by contracts.

2.—That State bonds and securities which cannot otherwise be
floated be purchased by the corporation when the proceeds of these
bonds and securities are to be used
for unemployment relief.

3.—That the corporation be
authorized to loan funds for self-
liquidating projects such as toll
bridges, tunnels and so forth.

ng the
rces of
orpora-
govern-
disburb-
pecting
uce for
he ...
finan-
are
ushing
e Cor-
can be

It provides that private business
planning reproductive enterprises for
which credit cannot be obtained from
the banks shall but put on a loaning
basis with the corporation, a plan
originally proposed by Mr. Hoover
when the corporation was created
but rejected by Congress.

au-
itional
,000 in
neral
r ac-

Senator Robinson, after a morning
conference with the President, called
a meeting of Democrats after the
Senate adjourned this afternoon and
outlined the President's idea. It was
favorably received.

Senator Watson talked to a number
of Republicans and reported progress
with the idea. Speaker Garner and
Minority Leader Snell were also con-
sulted, and tonight Republican members of the Senate Committee on
Banking and Currency were called to

Continued on Page Eleven.

# LINDBERGH BABY FOUND DEAD NEAR HOME; MURDERED SOON AFTER THE KIDNAPPING 72 DAYS AGO AND LEFT LYING IN WOOD:

## POLICE INTENSIFY HUNT

Curtis, Norfolk Agent,
and Condon, Who Paid
Ransom, at Hopewell.

## TO AID PROSECUTOR TODAY

Schwarzkopf Says Restraints
Designed to Safeguard Baby
Now Can Be Thrown Off.

## A GROUP UNDER SUSPICION

Gov. Moore Pledges Relentless
Hunt—Mulrooney Also
Promises Full Aid.

Dr. J. F. Condon, the Bronx lec-
turer who acted as intermediary in
the futile payment by Colonel Lindbergh of $50,000 ransom for his son,
and John H. Curtis, the Norfolk
boat-builder, who also has been con-
ducting negotiations, arrived at
Hopewell for questioning by the
police early this morning. They
were scheduled to go to the prose-
cutor's office in Mercer County later
today.

They arrived at the Lindbergh
home shortly before 5 o'clock this
morning and were at once closeted
with the police. A few minutes before their arrival Colonel H. Norman
Schwarzkopf, commanding the New
Jersey State Police, made this announcement:

"Dr. Condon and Mr. Curtis will
be at these headquarters in a few
minutes for questioning in connec-
tion with this case and they will be
turned over by the police authorities
at this point to the prosecuting authorities tomorrow morning."

**May Have Been Misled**

It is believed that the two inter-
mediaries may have confidential in-
formation about the kidnappers
which they are now ready to turn
over to the authorities.

With this announcement the head
of the New Jersey State Police indi-
cated that the hunt for the murderers
would be pursued with the aid of
State New York City and Federal
authorities, throwing off all the re-
straint that hitherto hampered the
police effort. It was disclosed further
by the New Jersey authorities that
immediate steps are being taken to

### WHERE KIDNAPPERS LEFT SLAIN BABY.

## SYMPATHY POURS IN FROM ALL THE WORLD

Grief and Horror Evidenced in
Capital Where Hoovers
Request Lindbergh News.

## ORTIZ RUBIO IS SADDENED

Messages Sent From Mexico
..ty—Inquiries Made From
London to Gov. Moore.

Widespread sympathy for the be-
reaved parents and relatives of
Charles A. Lindbergh Jr. and the
American people was expressed in
messages that poured into the Lindbergh home at Hopewell, N. J., last
night from various parts of the
world. Officials and civilians who
had hastened to join the international search for the kidnappers when
the abduction became known sought
to assuage the feelings they knew
would follow in the wake of the announcement.

The grief and horror with which
the nation received the fatal answer
in the question regarding the safety

## COLONEL BELIEVED ON A YACHT AT SEA

Reported Somewhere Off Block
Island on Search for the
Kidnappers.

## INFORMED OF BABY'S DEATH

Departed May 4 With Norfolk
Aides on Mission That Had
Seemed Promising.

Colonel Lindbergh was believed to
have been on a yacht, somewhere off
Block Island, when the body of his
son was discovered yesterday. He
had been there searching for the kidnappers of his son. There was no
question that he had learned of the
finding of the body, for Colonel H
Norman Schwarzkopf said that he
had been notified, and one of the
men with him—telephoning to Norfolk—said that the news had been
received.

Colonel Lindbergh set out from
Norfolk on May 4 on board the yacht
Marcon, owned by Charles H. Con-
solvo of Baltimore. With him were

## BODY MILE FROM HOPEWEL

Discovered by Chan
Near Centre of Wide
Search for Child.

### HALF-COVERED BY LEA

Skull Fractures Caused De
—Body and Clothing
Identified by Nurse.

### MOTHER IS BRAVE AT B

Neighbors Had Complained
Hunt in Vicinity Had N
Been Thorough.

The baby son of Colonel Char
Lindbergh was found dead yes
afternoon. The child had
murdered.

The body, lying face down in
pression and partly covere
dead leaves and wind-blown
was discovered by a Negro
driver, in a patch of woods
Sourland Mountains less th
miles from the Lindbergh hom
Hopewell, N. J.

The discovery was made
dent at 3:15 yesterday a
when the driver, walking
woods from the road, found
thought was a child's foot
out of the ground and not
police. The identification
quickly and the official
ment of the Lindbergh ba
was made at the Lindbergh

The child evidently had b
seen after he was stolen
crib in the nursery on the
March 1. Whether he h
killed with calculating pu
criminals who found it
geous to them to get rid o
or whether he had been th
by kidnappers fleeing in a
not determined last night.

**Two Fractures of**

The body showed the ma
fractures of the skull, one
side and the other on the

## FS ORT OUP

Senate 'Leg-
d.

## NEW RELIEF GROUP WITH SMITH AT HEAD NAMED BY WALKER

Merged Bureaus on Jobs and
Home Aid Have $5,000,000
to Use Until Aug. 1.

### UNITY OF EFFORT IS OBJECT

Copper
argo,

Leading Lawyers, Bankers and
Welfare Officials to Begin
Tasks on June 1.

Members of the Emergency Work
and Relief Administration, formed by
a consolidation of the Home Relief
Bureau and the Emergency Work
Commission, who will assume their
tasks on June 1 were notified of
their appointments yesterday by
Mayor Walker.

The new committee will consist of
the following

*Newspaper stories told the sad news.*

broken rung gave the police more clues. The police tested the ladder. Charles, Jr. weighed about 33 pounds (15 kg). A man of 150 to 179 pounds (68 to 81 kg) carrying the baby would have broken the ladder rung. The police decided the kidnapper was carrying Charles, Jr. down the ladder. The rung broke. They fell forward. The baby's head hit the wall of the house. This caused the child's death.

Also, the ladder had been made by a carpenter. Was the kidnapper a carpenter? One part of the ladder was special. The piece of wood had four clean nail holes. The board had been used for something else. Then it had been removed and put into the ladder. The wood had been inside a building. The nails would have rusted if the board had been outside. But no rust showed in the four holes.

The news about the baby's death and Condon's help appeared in the papers. Many people began to think that Condon was the kidnapper or part of the gang. Condon received angry letters. Some people said they would kill him.

Lindbergh wrote a letter to Condon. He

*The ladder used by the kidnapper was an important clue.*

thanked Condon for all his help. The letter was printed in many newspapers. Then people changed their thinking about Condon.

Meanwhile the ransom money was turning up in stores. New Jersey and New York City police questioned hundreds of people. But they were all innocent.

The New York Police Department used a special map of New York City. Wherever a bill from the ransom money was found, a colored pin was pushed into the map. Months and, finally, a year passed. More and more pins dotted the map.

The pins formed a spider web, with the Bronx in the middle. Police were now certain the kidnapper lived there. But the detectives could do nothing yet.

A year and a half went by.

During all this time, a wood expert named Arthur Koehler was working with the ladder. He knew that most of the ladder was pine wood. That type of pine grows in North Carolina and nearby states. There were marks in the wood made by a sawmill's knives. The knives were not working correctly. They made grooves. Koehler wrote 1,598 letters to southern sawmills. Had they repaired their knives lately?

Finally, one mill answered yes. Koehler tested some of their boards. The boards had the same grooves. Koehler got the names of all the wood supply companies in the New York City area. He visited each one that had bought wood from that mill. One company in the Bronx had bought southern pine from the mill. Koehler searched through thousands of receipts from that company. But he found no clues. The kidnapper may not have bought the wood there.

After months of work, Arthur Koehler was discouraged. His search only proved one fact. The kidnapper *could* have bought the wood from a company in the Bronx.

Policemen, detectives, and crime experts were working full time on the case. Every clue was checked. Newspapers said the police had messed up the case. But this was not true. Perhaps if they had worked harder at the beginning, they might have captured John. But Lindbergh had asked them to keep away until his son was safe.

Then good luck came their way. On September 15, 1934, a green car pulled into a New York City filling station. The driver paid his bill with a ten-dollar gold certificate. The clerk didn't see many of those any more. The government was changing to new money. He didn't want to be cheated with a fake bill. So he wrote the car's number on the bill. The bill was put in a bank.

A few days later, a bank teller was checking some money. The serial number showed that this bill was part of the ransom money. A note had been written on the bill. U-12-41, NY. Detectives found out that the bill had come from a filling station. The police went there and learned about the man in the green car. They checked with the Motor Vehicle Bureau. The car was owned by Bruno Richard Hauptmann, 1279 East 222nd Street, Bronx, New York. They learned that Hauptmann was a German. He was also a carpenter.

The police arrested Hauptmann. They found maps of New Jersey and Massachusetts in his house. Also, more than $14,000 of the ransom money had been hidden in Hauptmann's house and garage. Hauptmann said a friend had given

*Bruno Hauptmann was*
*arrested as a prime suspect.*

him the money. This friend had then gone back to Germany and had died there. There was no way Hauptmann could prove a friend had given him the money.

Charles Lindbergh came to the police station. The police had him wait outside a room. The door was slightly open. Lindbergh could not see into the room. Inside were a group of men. Each man would call out, "Here, Doctor." These were the words John had yelled the night he was given the ransom money. Lindbergh would never forget the voice of his son's kidnapper.

First, one man called, "Here, Doctor." Lindbergh shook his head no. Then another shouted. Again Lindbergh said that was not the voice. Suddenly Lindbergh heard the same voice he had heard before. That was the man. That was John. The suspect who had shouted was Bruno Richard Hauptmann.

More clues were found inside the Hauptmann house. Someone had written a telephone number on one of the inner walls. The number belonged to Condon. Also, Hauptmann read the Bronx

*Home News*. The paper was delivered each day to his house.

The police found another important clue in Hauptmann's attic. A board had been removed from the floor. The wood matched a rung in the ladder. The rung fit into the floor. There were nail holes in the rung and the floor. They matched.

Bruno Hauptmann's trial was held in New Jersey. Thousands crowded into the small town.

Charles Lindbergh was at the trial. Anne Lindbergh was too upset to be there. She came only to testify. At times, the people inside the court could not hear what was being said. Outside, the mob was screaming, "Kill Hauptmann, kill Hauptmann."

The trial lasted six weeks. Hauptmann was found guilty of murder. He was put to death on April 3, 1936. This was a little more than four years after the kidnapping.

Anna Hauptmann says her husband did not kidnap the baby. Bruno Hauptmann never confessed to the crime. But the evidence was strong against him.

There are questions which have never been answered. How did Hauptmann know which room the baby was in? Did someone help Hauptmann? What about the Italian voice Condon heard on the phone when speaking to John? Why did Hauptmann keep saying and writing "we"?

Bruno Richard Hauptmann knew the answers to those questions. But he is dead. Perhaps we will never learn all the truth about the Lindbergh kidnapping.

# CHAPTER 4

# THE

# MYSTERY

# OF

# FLIGHT

The night of November 15, 1959, was a warm one in Florida. The sky was clear.

At Miami Airport, Flight 967 was already a half hour late. This flight was to go to Tampa, New Orleans, Dallas, and end in Los Angeles.

The plane flew from Miami to Tampa and landed to pick up more passengers. Several strange things happened that night in Tampa.

A man about 6 feet (1.8 m) tall came into the terminal. He was in his sixties and had white hair. The skin under his chin formed a pouch. He had a ticket for Flight 967.

A clerk took his suitcase and stamped the ticket. "Gate One," he said. "The flight is about thirty minutes late tonight."

The man took back his ticket and boarding pass. He then left the terminal. No one knows if he came back. Other passengers for Flight 967 did arrive. Soon all the Tampa passengers were in the waiting room.

At first no one noticed one special person in the group. He wore a dark hat and brown coat. He went into a tobacco shop.

Pulling a dollar bill from his pocket, he asked, "May I have four quarters, please?"

The clerk gave him the change. She watched as he went to a flight insurance machine. Then she went to help another customer.

A call came over the airport loudspeaker. Flight 967 was now ready. The man in the brown coat rushed to Gate Fourteen. A clerk there told him that he wanted Gate One. That was his Dallas flight. The man hurried toward the correct plane.

At 12:39 A.M., Flight 967 moved along the runway. Weather was clear for all the airports where the plane would land. The pilot, Captain Frank E. Todd, checked the engines. Everything was working fine. The plane was cleared for take-off by the tower. The aircraft rolled down the runway and lifted off the ground. There were forty-two passengers on board.

All planes must radio Air Route Traffic Control during a flight. At 1:05 A.M., Captain Todd made his first report. Todd checked a weather report at 1:31 A.M. The plane was also being tracked by radar. First, a radar screen in Alabama showed the speck which was Flight 967. Then a second station in Louisiana showed a dot on the screen. Flight 967 was moving ahead well.

Not far from the Louisiana radar station, Richard Prince watched the sky. Prince was on duty in a Coast Guard tower.

Suddenly, the sky lit up with a bright flash. The light was yellow-red and seemed the size of the sun. This flash lasted only a few seconds. Then came a bright white light which fell to the water. The sky turned dark again. Prince wondered what had caused the light. He had never seen a falling star like that before. He checked his watch. The time was 1:50 A.M.

At the same time, the people in the radar station were puzzled. A moment before they had been watching Flight 967 on the screen. The speck had turned sharply to the left. Then it disappeared. The radar crew wrote the fact in their records. The time was 1:51 A.M.

At 2:06 A.M., the control tower tried to contact the plane by radio. Captain Todd did not answer. Two minutes later another call went out.

*Robert Spears had a police record
dating back to the 1920s.*

Then another call was made one minute later. Flight 967 still did not reply. The airplane had vanished only ten minutes before it would have landed in New Orleans.

Rescue missions were sent to hunt for the plane. While this was being done, the airline checked the passenger list. One of the passengers was Carol Taylor from Oklahoma. Someone would have to call her family. Another passenger was Ellis "Itchy" Mandel. He was a friend of a well-known gangster named Mickey Cohen. Dr. R. Spears was listed as a passenger going from Tampa to Dallas.

Robert Spears was born in Missouri on June 26, 1894. He would be known by several names in his lifetime. As a young man, he sold fake medicine. When he was twenty-two, he was arrested for jewel robbery. In 1925, he was charged with mail fraud. He was sent to jail for six months. Arrested with him was a friend named William Allen Taylor.

Nine years later, Spears was again caught by the police. This time it was for forgery. He spent a year in prison. When he was set free, he went to Florida to join Al Taylor. The men formed a crooked business. They collected money and said it would be given to good causes. Secretly, they kept the money for themselves. They were arrested and sent to a Florida prison.

Spears and Taylor were released one year later. They moved north to Baltimore, Maryland. Less than two weeks later, they were jailed for forgery.

Both men were let out on parole after two years. Taylor returned to Tampa, Florida, and married Alice Steele. He never broke the law again.

But Robert Spears suddenly became Dr. Robert Vernon Spears. He never studied medicine. He just called himself a doctor. He went to Dallas and soon had many patients. Frances Massey became his secretary and then his girl friend.

Spears had not gone to Al Taylor's wedding. He decided now to give a gift to the Taylors. He invited them to a fancy St. Petersburg, Florida, hotel. They all stayed there for four days. Spears bought expensive dinners for them.

Alice Taylor did not like her husband'

friend. At first she did not know why. Then she understood the reason. Al was like Spears's slave. If Spears wanted a drink, Al jumped to his feet and made one. Al Taylor loved to discuss anything from baseball to politics. But whatever Spears said, Al agreed with. Al was acting like a little boy near his big hero. By the time Spears left Florida, Alice could not hide her dislike for him.

On December 22, 1950, Robert Spears married Frances Massey. Al Taylor flew from Florida to be the best man. One of the guests was Dr. William A. Turska. Spears had met Turska at a medical meeting. Dr. Turska's wife Ann did not like Spears. But she did not make that fact known as Alice Taylor did.

On November 15, 1959, Al Taylor was in the Hillsboro Hotel in Tampa. Al Taylor's son came to the room. He saw Al talking with a white-haired man who had a flabby pouch under his chin. The man was his father's old friend, Dr. Robert Spears.

No one knows what the two men talked about in the hotel. But that night a man who looked like Spears checked a suitcase for Flight 967. He then

*Searchers found few traces of
Flight 967 floating in the water.*

left the terminal. Another man who looked like Taylor bought flight insurance. He then tried to board the wrong plane. He was sent to Flight 967.

The search planes and boats had trouble finding any trace of Flight 967. Low clouds had moved into the area. Finally, a search plane saw objects in the water. There were pillows, an empty life raft, and several bodies. Many of the dead passengers had already been eaten by sharks. There was oil on the water. Clothing had been ripped off the bodies. This might mean that the plane had hit the water with great force. This might also mean that the plane had exploded.

Everyone wondered why the pilot had not said that the plane was in trouble. Even in mid-air crashes, pilots have had time to send a message. Flight 967 had been silent. The F.B.I. and other people began to think that the plane had blown up. The gangster, Mandel, was on the plane. An enemy might have put a bomb aboard to kill him. Parts of the plane were found over a wide area. This might mean that the plane was in pieces before hitting the water. Pillows and suitcases inside the plane had burn marks. But no one could tell yet if the plane had blown up before or after the crash. Divers were sent underwater to find the plane itself.

One clue was found in a flight attendant's body. Doctors studied how her leg bones were broken. The bones showed she had been walking at the time of the explosion. Nine people had been seated but had not been wearing seat belts. If the plane had been coming down, things would have been different. People would have had their seat-belts on. The flight attendant would have been sitting or lying on the floor. It seemed that the plane had exploded in the air.

Searchers hunted for the plane. F.B.I. agents tried to track down any enemies of "Itchy" Mandel.

Alice Taylor was worried. Al and she were now divorced. But they were still good friends. Al had come to see her the night that Flight 967 had crashed. He had told her he was leaving for Atlanta, Georgia. He was going to see about a job. He had seemed nervous.

The next night Alice had played cards with

friends. The group had met in her house. She had read the news about the plane crash. But this meant little to her. Then her son, William, came into the house.

"Mom," he said, "do you know who was on that plane?"

"The one that crashed?" she asked.

"Doctor Spears. It lists him here." The seventeen-year-old boy held up a newspaper.

Her first thought was to call Al. She did not like Spears but she knew Al would be upset. Al had said he would be gone one day. That meant he would be flying to Atlanta. But what if he had gone to Dallas? Alice knew that Al would do anything and go anywhere for Spears. She read the passengers' names in the newspaper. She caught her breath. The name Taylor was there. But that was Carol Taylor from Oklahoma.

Her son tried to calm her. "They know there were only forty-two persons on board. And they have all of their names."

Alice Taylor was still worried. She tried to call Al several times. No one answered his phone.

*Alice Taylor was too worried to sleep.*

She and her son drove to Tampa Airport. They searched the parking lot. But they did not find Al's car. Nor was the car parked outside his dark apartment.

She was awake most of the night. If Al had flown somewhere, he would have parked his car at the airport. He must have come back. Yet he wasn't home. Nor had he called to talk about Spears's death.

The next day she called his apartment every hour. Still no answer to the ringing telephone. She called his place of work. People there said they had expected him the day before.

Alice Taylor wondered if she should call the police. But they might think she was being silly. Instead, she talked to Al's boss, Robert Christie, and asked him what to do.

Christie said he would phone the Missing Persons Bureau. The Bureau sent out a report about Al Taylor. He would be driving his salmon-and-white 1957 Plymouth sedan.

A week passed. Alice Taylor went to the Tampa police. She told them that she was sure Al had been on Flight 967. The police checked with the airline. Every passenger was known. All had relatives or friends. There were no extra people on the flight.

Leaving the police station, Alice and her son went to Al's apartment. The landlord let them into the apartment. Only one suit was missing from the place. Also, his brown coat and hat were gone. Yet, his razor and shaving cream were on a shelf. Why hadn't he taken those things to Atlanta? Wherever he had gone, he had not planned to stay long.

Alice went to the post office. But she needed a court order to get Al's mail. Her lawyer took care of that. There was one special letter addressed to her son. Alice Taylor saw her ex-husband's handwriting on the long envelope.

Inside was a flight insurance policy for $37,500. Her son, William Allen Taylor, Jr., would get the money. The policy had been bought ten minutes before Flight 967 had left Tampa. The owner was going to Dallas. Al Taylor had bought the insurance policy. Alice knew Al's writing.

She called the airline. She said Al must have been using Spears's name. The airline called the F.B.I. and asked them to check this new fact.

Alice Taylor also told her story to a Tampa newspaper. She claimed Al had been hypnotized by Spears. She thought Spears had told Al to take his place on the plane. The crazy-sounding story was printed in other newspapers. A Dallas newspaper also gave space to the story. A radio news chief saw the story. Eddie Barker was his name. Barker visited Spears's wife, Frances, with his tape recorder.

Frances Spears was recovering from her grief. At first she had been so upset she could do nothing. Then she had to get her husband's business papers in order. She told Barker she had found Spears's will. Everything was left to Frances. But she needed proof he had died. She had written to the airline. They sent a paper which said Spears was on the passenger list. At first the court would not accept that paper. Finally a lawyer convinced the court that Spears was dead.

None of these people in Tampa or Dallas

*William Turska's cabin seemed a
good hideout for Spears.*

knew an important fact. The F.B.I. was widening its search. They were now hunting for Al Taylor and Taylor's car and Robert Spears. They had learned some new facts. A short time before the crash, Spears had bought a $100,000 flight insurance policy. Also, Spears knew about explosives. F.B.I. agents began thinking about Alice Taylor's story. Had Spears sent Taylor on the plane? Had Spears put a bomb in the suitcase?

There were other unanswered questions. If Taylor had not been on Flight 967, where was he? If Taylor was dead, where was Spears? And where was Taylor's car?

The missing car and Robert Spears were in Arizona. Spears was living in a cabin owned by William Turska. Life had not gone well for Turska in the years he had known Spears. Turska and his wife, Ann, had moved to Phoenix, Arizona. Turska was arrested for doing illegal abortions. He also began drinking and was drunk much of the time. Ann had divorced him.

Turska's cabin was far from town in the desert foothills. A man who lived near the cabin saw

Spears and the car. This man did not know the F.B.I. was looking for both. In fact, he had not heard about Flight 967.

About six weeks after the crash of Flight 967, William Turska went to Dallas. He visited Frances Spears's house. He took her to the Lakewood Hotel in Dallas. There she learned shocking news.

"I thought Doctor Spears was dead, and there he was in front of me," she later said.

Turska left. Frances Spears claimed that she begged the doctor to go to the police. He said no. He wanted to collect the $100,000 insurance money. In the days after the meeting, Frances Spears would not see any reporters.

Meanwhile, Turska drove Spears back to Arizona. During the trip, Spears rested his hand on Turska's shoulder. "It's good for a man to have a close friend. You have done so much for me. I'd like to do something for you."

"Forget it."

"No. Have you ever been to Hawaii?" Spears asked.

"No."

"You're going there as my guest," Spears told him. "I'll buy the plane tickets for you."

Turska said no. But he was pleased. At this time Turska and Frances both believed the plane crash was an accident. Later Turska would wonder about Spears's offer.

An odd thing took place a few weeks later. It would change the case of Flight 967. The ex-wife of William Turska was in Phoenix. She saw Robert Spears crossing a street. She remembered him well from the time he visited her ex-husband. She had heard he was dead. Then she had read that the F.B.I. was looking for him.

Spears walked past Ann Turska without seeing her. The woman knew the F.B.I. would want to know about this. She told the agents she had seen Spears alive. She also told them about Turska's cabin.

Several days later, William Turska was worried. There was a workman on a telephone pole, fixing the wires. He had been there a very long time. Also, during the last few days, several cars had gone past the cabin. That was strange. Per-

*Spears stayed in the car while Turska
rented a motel room for him.*

haps one car would come along in a month. Now more cars than usual were seen.

Even as he watched, another car went by. It drove up the road and then came back. Turska told Spears that the cars might belong to the police. Turska had his lawyer check the number of the last car he had seen. The car was owned by an undercover detective.

William Turska brought Spears to the Bali Hi Motel in Phoenix. He rented a room while Spears stayed in the car. Spears was wearing a heavy coat. The collar was turned up. No one could see his face. Turska told the clerk that his friend had the flu. After Spears went to his room, Turska left the motel. The F.B.I. captured him soon after.

At noon the next day, the motel desk clerk had a surprise. A man came to the desk wearing a brown coat and a checkered cap. He had a rope slung around his neck. On each end hung a suitcase.

The man said, "I'm checking out."

He put down twenty dollars. A taxi pulled up outside. The man got his change and ran to the cab. He threw his suitcases into the trunk. The taxi moved a few feet and then stopped for a light. Suddenly, two men were there. One went to each side of the taxi. They pulled open the doors and dragged out Robert Spears.

In Spears's suitcases were electrical tape, flashlight batteries, and blasting caps. The F.B.I. also found dynamite in Turska's cabin. Turska had not known about that. Spears had everything needed to make a bomb. But he said he did not bomb Flight 967. He could only be charged with having illegal explosives.

Spears stuck to one story no matter how often he was questioned. He said Taylor had begged him for his airline ticket. Taylor was sick and needed treatment in Dallas. Spears had only done a good deed. He had given his ticket to a friend. Of course, he said, he was very unhappy about what happened to Al Taylor.

Spears said the crash had been a good chance for him. He could stay hidden. He could start a new life without a criminal record. Also, his family would benefit from the money.

Even while Spears was being questioned, ships hunted for what was left of the plane. They found many wrecks. But they did not find Flight 967. So Spears could not be charged with bombing the plane.

Robert Spears was charged under the federal Dyer Act. That law says a person cannot drive a car into another state without the owner's permission. Spears admitted he was guilty. He was sent to Alcatraz Prison in San Francisco for five years. He was never brought to trial for bombing Flight 967.

Did Robert Spears place a bomb on the plane? Did he kill forty-two people? Or did something else such as lightning cause the crash? We will never know for sure. The wreckage of Flight 967 is still under the muddy waters of the Gulf of Mexico.

# INDEX

[85]

# Outstanding Laurel-Leaf Fiction
# for Young Adult Readers

☐ **A LITTLE DEMONSTRATION OF AFFECTION**
*Elizabeth Winthrop* $1.25
A 15-year-old girl and her older brother find themselves turning
to each other to share their deepest emotions.

☐ **M.C. HIGGINS THE GREAT**
*Virginia Hamilton* $1.50
Winner of the Newbery Medal, the National Book Award and
the Boston Globe-Horn Book Award, this novel follows M.C.
Higgins' growing awareness that both choice and action lie
within his power.

☐ **PORTRAIT OF JENNIE**
*Robert Nathan* $1.25
Robert Nathan interweaves touching and profound portraits of
all his characters with one of the most beautiful love stories
ever told.

☐ **THE MEAT IN THE SANDWICH**
*Alice Bach* $1.50
Mike Lefcourt dreams of being a star athlete, but when hockey
season ends, Mike learns that victory and defeat become
hopelessly mixed up.

☐ **Z FOR ZACHARIAH**
*Robert C. O'Brien* $1.50
This winner of an Edgar Award from the Mystery Writers of
America portrays a young girl who was the only human being
left alive after nuclear doomsday—or so she thought.